Greater Than a Tourist Boc

MW00891044

I think the series is wonderful and beneficial for tourists to get information before visiting the city.

-Seckin Zumbul, Izmir Turkey

I am a world traveler who has read many trip guides but this one really made a difference for me. I would call it a heartfelt creation of a local guide expert instead of just a guide.

-Susy, Isla Holbox, Mexico

New to the area like me, this is a must have!

-Joe, Bloomington, USA

This is a good series that gets down to it when looking for things to do at your destination without having to read a novel for just a few ideas.

-Rachel, Monterey, USA

Good information to have to plan my trip to this destination.

-Pennie Farrell, Mexico

Aptly titled, you won't just be a tourist after reading this book. You'll be greater than a tourist!

-Alan Warner, Grand Rapids, USA

Thank you for a fantastic book.

-Don, Philadelphia, USA

D.R. Perry

Great ideas for a port day.
-Mary Martin USA

Even though I only have three days to spend in San Miguel in an upcoming visit, I will use the author's suggestions to guide some of my time there. An easy read - with chapters named to guide me in directions I want to go.
-Robert Catapano, USA

Great insights from a local perspective! Useful information and a very good value!
-Sarah, USA

This series provides an in-depth experience through the eyes of a local. Reading these series will help you to travel the city in with confidence and it'll make your journey a unique one.
-Andrew Teoh, Ipoh, Malaysia

Tourists can get an amazing "insider scoop" about a lot of places from all over the world. While reading, you can feel how much love the writer put in it.
-Vanja Živković, Sremski Karlovci, Serbia

GREATER THAN A TOURIST— PROVIDENCE RHODE ISLAND USA

50 Travel Tips from a Local

D.R. Perry

D.R. Perry

Greater Than a Tourist
Visit our website at www.GreaterThanaTourist.com

Lock Haven, PA

ISBN: 9781973438021

>TOURIST

50 TRAVEL TIPS FROM A LOCAL

D.R. Perry

BOOK DESCRIPTION

Are you excited about planning your next trip?

Do you want to try something new?

Would you like some guidance from a local?

If you answered yes to any of these questions, then this Greater Than a Tourist book is for you.

Greater Than a Tourist—Providence Rhode Island USA by D.R. Perry offers the inside scoop on Providence. Most travel books tell you how to travel like a tourist. Although there is nothing wrong with that, as part of the Greater Than a Tourist series, this book will give you travel tips from someone who has lived at your next travel destination.

In these pages you'll discover advice that will help you throughout your stay. This book will not tell you exact addresses or store hours but instead will give you excitement and knowledge from a local that you may not find in other smaller print travel books.

Travel like a local. Slow down, stay in one place, and get to know the people and the culture. By the time you finish this book, you will be eager and prepared to travel to your next destination.

D.R. Perry

TABLE OF CONTENTS

17. Providence Children's Museum
18. Shop Providence Place Mall
19. Visit The Arcade
20. Rhode Island ComiCon
21. Get Coffee Milk
22. Del's Frozen Lemonade
23. Chow On Clam Cakes and Chowder
24. Take A Walk In The Park
25. Get Spooked In Providence
26. Try The Calamari
27. Get On The Local Tap
28. Make A State Visit
29. Fascinating Fall Foliage
30. The Providence Performing Arts Center
31. Dunkin Donuts Center
32. Try Trinity Reperatory Theatre
33. Fine Art: The Festival Ballet
34. Visit Art Galleries
35. Fun Times At Foo Fest
36. Align With NecronomiCon
37. See The Summer Concert Series
38. Ride A Gondola
39. Providence Artisans Market
40. Hope Street Farmer's Market
41. Walking On Waterplace
42. Dining On The Water
43. Take A Lighthouse Cruise
44. Check Out Historic Churches
45. Travel By The Providence Train Station

DEDICATION

This book is dedicated to my husband. I love Rhode Island but never would have given this quirky little state a chance if I hadn't loved him first.

D.R. Perry

ABOUT THE AUTHOR

D.R. Perry is an author who lives in and writes about Rhode Island. Her series include the Young Adult Paranormal Humor series, Providence Paranormal College and the Decopunk Alternate History Quartet, La Famiglia di Mostri. This is her first work of non-fiction, though she has a series of cookbooks in the works.

She shares time and space with her husband, their daughter, and their little dog, too. D.R. loves Rhode Island because, like her, it looks small but contains so much.

D.R. Perry

HOW TO USE THIS BOOK

The Greater Than a Tourist book series was written by someone who has lived in an area for over three months. The goal of this book is to help travelers either dream or experience different locations by providing opinions from a local. The author has made suggestions based on their own experiences. Please do your own research before traveling to the area in case the suggested places are unavailable.

D.R. Perry

FROM THE PUBLISHER

Traveling can be one of the most important parts of a person's life. The anticipation and memories that you have are some of the best. As a publisher of the Greater Than a Tourist book series, as well as the popular 50 Things to Know book series, we strive to help you learn about new places, spark your imagination, and inspire you. Wherever you are and whatever you do I wish you safe, fun, and inspiring travel.

Lisa Rusczyk Ed. D.
CZYK Publishing

D.R. Perry

OUR STORY

Traveling is a passion of the "Greater than a Tourist" series creator. Lisa studied abroad in college, and for their honeymoon Lisa and her husband toured Europe. During her travels to Malta, an older man tried to give her some advice based on his own experience living on the island since he was a young boy. She was not sure if she should talk to the stranger but was interested in his advice. When traveling to some places she was wary to talk to locals because she was afraid that they weren't being genuine. Through her travels, Lisa learned how much locals had to share with tourists. Lisa created the "Greater Than a Tourist" book series to help connect people with locals. A topic that locals are very passionate about sharing.

D.R. Perry

WELCOME TO
> TOURIST

D.R. Perry

INTRODUCTION

"Why do you go away? So that you can come back. So that you can see the place you came from with new eyes and extra colors."–Terry Pratchett

Moving to Rhode Island was a confusing experience. I'd been in the state just to pass through on the way to and from New York City, occasionally stopping for a bathroom break. Little did I know it'd be my future home.

It's been twelve years since then. I'm comfortable with the city's unique lingo, its quirks. The city of Providence used to feel like the sort of temporary friend you make at an airport. Now it's like that friend whose house feels like a second home.

D.R. Perry

There's more to the biggest city in the smallest state than you can see in one weekend or even a whole month. This guide will help you whatever your length of stay. The first three points are the most important if you're only in Providence for a few days or less

I mention a few things that only happen seasonally but that's pretty typical for any state in the northeastern United States. Though you will hear locals complain about the weather, we secretly love it because it's never boring. Just like Rhode Island itself. I'm so glad you've picked up this book to help plan your visit. Rhode Island is one of the most interesting places I've ever been to and I feel lucky to share it with you.

1. THE AIRPORT IS NOT IN PROVIDENCE

If you're flying in, remember that our friendly little airport is in the town of Warwick. This is about a ten minute drive from Providence and a half hour on the city bus. Some hotels have free shuttles to the city but not all. Call them to make sure.

The airport area has several hotels. Most of them are nice but they're not in Providence. Staying in one of these means you'll have to either rent a car of depend on someone else to drive you up to the city every day. If you want to get the real experience, book a hotel in the city so you can simply walk outside to begin your adventures there.

There's so much to see and do in Providence and traffic to and from the airport can be heavy. Getting to Providence from Warwick only takes time better spent seeing the sights, having a meal, or enjoying local art.

2. HOW TO GET DIRECTIONS IN PROVIDENCE

Be careful asking locals for directions in the city. Everyone's much friendlier than the folks up in Boston but they tend to get confusing when asked where something is. It's nothing personal, just how Rhode Islanders have learned to navigate.

Imagine asking where City Hall is and being told "the Superman building is past the third Dunks, across the street from where Cardi's used to be back in the seventies." If you are extra adventurous, maybe you could try navigating by that description. I tried it myself when I first visited here and got lost. Luckily, everyone in the coffee shop I stopped in banded together to help me because the people are so nice.

If it's your first time in Providence, a phone with data will help you immensely. Try to get the address for places you want to visit online or during your stay. You can put these into Google Maps or Wayz and find everything with ease.

3. DUNKIN' DONUTS IS A LANDMARK

Coffee is part of the culture in Providence. You'll see lots of places to get it, from chains like Starbucks or Dunkin' to unique local shops like The Coffee Exchange and Bolt Coffee.

Unless you drink coffee several times a day, don't bother getting your caffeine fix there. With so many unique places to have your cup of Joe, you could visit a different café every day for two weeks. The independent coffee shops also give you a place to rest and get your bearings. Bonus for you, they all have Wi-Fi.

One of the literally cool things you will notice are a majority of locals drinking iced coffee in the middle of the winter. When I first moved here, I thought it was the strangest thing ever until I tried it myself. Even so, the quirk stuck with me so firmly, I put it in one of my fiction novels. You might do a double-take like I did but maybe you'll be brave and try your coffee "on the rocks" in winter.

4. ART IS EVERYWHERE YOU LOOK

You can hardly turn a corner in any section of Providence without seeing an original creation. One of the best things about this city is its quirkiness and the public art displays go along with that.

Waterplace Park has a tile mural inside an underpass. Thayer Street has a vibrant mural. Artistic embellishments grace the doorways and eaves of buildings throughout the city. Statues stand in city squares, ranging from state founders to literary greats.

With the Rhode Island School of Design and art programs at every college in the state, evidence of creativity is everywhere. Even if you don't plan to visit any galleries or shows, visual masterpieces are just parts of the landscape here. Don't forget to stop and appreciate the views, both large and small.

5. PLAN SOME TIME FOR WATERFIRE

Speaking of Waterplace Park, for half the year, it's on fire. Don't worry that's intentional. The city has an event every Saturday where volunteers light braziers anchored to the riverbed. That sounds like something worth seeing all by itself but there's more to our festival than that.

WaterFire is basically a huge street party. It's in the city center and includes live entertainment, food trucks, and souvenir vendors. In the warm summer months, the streets are packed with people enjoying the sights and sounds. Even in the chillier seasons you will see locals and tourists alike taking in the festivities.

Be prepared for some delays when navigating Providence if you're trying to get somewhere else during WaterFire. Traffic cops help direct pedestrians across busy intersections on Memorial Boulevard but even so it takes more time than normal to get around while either walking or driving. If you leave the city center before five o'clock and return after eleven, you can avoid the traffic.

6. THE BEST PIZZA IN PROVIDENCE

When it comes to pizza, we're definitely not New York but there are some restaurants where pizza is as much an art form as the art around town. Even if you're in Providence for a day trip, you have to try the pizza in this town.

When it comes to oven-baked comfort food, there are two schools of thought—thin crust and deep piles of gooey bread. Guess which one I prefer? We have both here, so don't worry if we disagree.

I'm naming two places with different styles but a walk through almost anywhere in Providence will lead to great pizza if you follow your nose. The greatest cheese masterpieces can be found at Caserta's in Federal Hill and Al Forno in Fox Point. You can read more about those parts of the city in tips nine and eleven.

7. NY SYSTEM IS NOT FOR TRANSIT

You might hear the phrase "let's get some wieners" while walking around in Providence. They're not talking about Oscar Mayer here; they mean New York System or "hot wieners."

They're like second cousins to a chili dog—red skin, shorter than the regular length ones you can buy at grocery stores. The biggest difference is in the toppings. NY System dogs are topped with spiced meat, mustard, and chopped onion.

Most locals will tell you it's a crime to add anything else to a wiener but the shops typically have condiments such as ketchup, barbecue sauce, malted vinegar, and celery salt available. The die-hard fans say these are for when you get fries on the side.

This is probably the most locally unique food in the state of Rhode Island. You can't find this stuff over the border in Massachusetts or Connecticut, so get it while you're here if you want to try it.

8. RHODE ISLAND HAS ISLANDS

You might hear people say "we're not an island and not Long Island" about our state. Rhode Island isn't actually separated from the mainland by the ocean. However, it does have two islands.

Aquidneck Island is connected to the state by two bridges, in the middle of the Bay and home to Newport. That's a whole different destination on its own. I could write a whole different guide about it (and probably will some other time). There's plenty to do and see year-round.

If you listen to the radio while in Providence, you might hear advertisements encouraging you to "sail away on the Block Island Ferry." That's the only way to get there unless you own a small aircraft, by the way. It's very seasonal, with nearly no events over the winter and sparse offerings in Fall and Spring.

9. EXPLORE FEDERAL HILL

Rhode Island's Italian culture is at its best in this section of Providence. Locals often refer to it as "The Hill," and it's both a must-see and must-dine location. Coming down Atwells Avenue from downtown, you'll pass under a landmark we call LaPigna. It looks like a giant pineapple but is actually a pinecone, which means high quality. It makes sense for this to symbolize the neighborhood.

Federal Hill is home to historic buildings, monuments, and some of the best restaurants in the entire state. If you plan on having any Italian food, this is where you want to find a restaurant.

If you're driving, park and walk around. Find Southern Italian cuisine at Siena or Northern at Trattoria Zooma. For dessert, walk down De Pasquale Square for one block toward Pastiche and Café Dolce Vita.

The Hill has an upscale night life scene, too. From cocktail lounges like Zara to cigar bars like Da Vinci. Not looking for Italian? That's okay. There are other options, like Lucia's Mexican, Bombay Club for Indian, and even Nami's for Japanese cuisine.

10. CLIMB COLLEGE HILL

This neighborhood is accurately named as home to Brown University, Rhode Island School of Design, and Bryant University. This area has much to offer, from scenic parks to restaurants and shopping. The Brown University campus also has several sights to see.

College Hill is one of the best examples of Historic Preservation in the United States. The Fleur De Lys Studio, John Brown House, and Providence Athenaeum are all must-see examples of the eclectic architecture here. Remember when I said art is everywhere in Providence? It's doubly true on College Hill.

Prospect Terrace Park is the place to go if you want a chance to take a panoramic photo of Providence. It's set high on the hillside overlooking the city. You can get a great shot of City Hall's roof from there. At night, take a walk down Thayer Street to see the bright lights on the marquee at the Avon Cinema.

Thayer Street is home to locally owned shops and casual eateries of almost every type. Grab a falafel sandwich to walk with at East Side Pockets and dessert at La Creperie. For a sit-down meal, try Kabob and Curry or Café Paragon.

11. FIND FOX POINT

Fox Point is a great place to go if you want to be by the water. It's home to India Point Park as well as streets full of eclectic shopping, dining, and architecture.

To get to the park from Wickenden Street, you have to cross Interstate 95. There's a pedestrian bridge made especially for that and up top is a great place to snap a few photos of the Bay. India Point Park has an amphitheater and hosts musical events during warmer months. Check local listings for specific dates and artist information.

One of the best dive bars in the city is Wickenden Pub on the street of the same name. You'll find places to get all kinds of food, coffee, and even tea with desserts at the Duck and Bunny.

Services abound here, too. You could get your nails done, eyebrows threaded, or tattoo inked. If you're more interested in shopping, there's Round Again Records with the best vinyl selection in Southern New England, an aquarium shop, and several antique collections to pick through, from upscale to novelty.

12. VISIT HOPE VILLAGE

You can explore so much in Hope. If you love historic buildings, check out the Lippitt House Museum. Brown University's Ladd Observatory is open to the public.

Excellent restaurants are literally on every block of Hope Street. Tortilla Flats, Wings Over Providence, and Seven Stars Bakery are all on the eastern end with India, Ran Zan, and Three Sisters to the west near the Cemetery. You can hit the Blackstone Valley Walking Trail if you want to work off some of those calories.

No visit to the East Side is complete without a visit to Swan Point Cemetery. You can visit the graves of Roger Williams and H. P. Lovecraft. Make sure you have a look during daylight hours, though, because security is strict after dark.

13. THE INFAMOUS AWFUL AWFUL

Want to look and sound like the locals while visiting an ice cream parlor? Never order a milkshake. In Providence, that means milk in a glass with syrup and ice cubes, shaken like James Bond's favorite martini.

If you've got a craving for the tasty beverage made from ice cream, milk, and flavored syrup, you want to order a frappe. Up in Massachusetts, they also say cabinet so they'll know what you mean if you order one of those, too. But you shouldn't go just anywhere for your frozen beverage fix.

There's one frappe that stands above the rest in Providence, available at Newport Creamery. It's the Awful Awful, which is short for "awful big, awful good." They come in just about any flavor you can imagine. On Mondays, you can buy one of these twenty-four ounce drinkable confections and get one free.

14. HEAR SOME LOCAL MUSIC

Providence's own Alternative music station went off the radio airwaves in the middle of 2017. Don't worry, they're still going strong as a streaming station and supporting the local indie bands we've come to know and love in the Ocean State. They still sponsor and broadcast all kinds of events which you can read more about throughout this book.

Local music plays at a number of venues every day of most weeks. Check the Providence Journal or walk right up to one of the venues. Lupo's, AS220, The Spot, The Met and Firehouse 13 all give a chance for Rhode Island bands to play. National and even worldwide acts also come through, so check listings to see what's playing while you're in town.

Musical acts that got their start in Providence include Deer Tick, The Amazing Royal Crowns, Draco and the Malfoys, Vital Remains, and Blu Cantrell. Our scene has a diverse style.

15. LOVECRAFT AND THE LITERARY SCENE

Rhode Island is like a magnet for writers. H. P. Lovecraft, one of the classic authors in the Horror genre, wrote most of his work here. We've also got a state professional organization called ARIA; the Rhode Island Association of Authors.

There are open mic nights, poetry slams, workshops and write-ins in Providence, as well as a new bookstore full of locally written works just over the line in Pawtucket.

This city is an inspiring place. I wrote ten fiction novels that take place in Providence just because of how interesting a setting I thought it would be. Maybe you'll get bitten by the creativity bug during your stay, too. Locals love reading books that take place in the Ocean State. If you write one, be sure to let us know.

16. ROGER WILLIAMS ZOO: IT'S A JUNGLE IN THERE

If you're in Providence for more than a day or two, you absolutely must visit the zoo. It's got something for everyone, with multiple exhibits of exotic animals and even a petting zoo with farm animals for the kids.

During October, they also have a Jack-O-Lantern Spectacular event with hundreds of carved pumpkins on display after dark. Be sure to bundle up if it's cold; you'll want plenty of time to walk through and see these spooky creations.

Other events happen after dark at the Zoo. Check their website to find out the schedule for drinking or dining events. Brew at the Zoo is a blast! Many of these are for charity to help the Zoo, so you can feel good about attending for more than one reason.

17. PROVIDENCE CHILDREN'S MUSEUM

Even if you don't have the kids with you, you still might want to consider a visit to the Children's Museum. Its exhibits range from basic science demonstrations and activities to local history about art, entertainment, and industry. The second floor holds fascinating interactive displays depicting the daily life of Providence residents across different time periods.

Seasonal cultural exhibits are rich and varied, with content and presentation appropriate for children and of interest to adults. Check the museum's website for the latest exhibit information. Admission is free from five to eight at night on the third Friday of every month.

The museum is down the street from Rhode Island Hospital so parking can be difficult. It might be worthwhile to take a bus or call a car.

18. SHOP PROVIDENCE PLACE MALL

If shopping is one of the things you love about travel, Providence Place is a must-see. With three stories, anchor restaurants, a bar with a gaming arcade, and even an IMAX movie theater, you can spend the entire day at this mall.

All the usual shops for men's, women's, and children's fashion are there, lining the concourse between Macy's and Nordstrom. Specialty shops like the Lego store and Newbury Comics add an element of fun.

The mall has an attached parking lot, so it's easy to get a convenient place to park if you're driving. If not, don't worry. The mall is across the street from Kennedy Plaza, a bus station that happens to be the hub of most public transit in the state. Uber, Lyft, and taxi drivers all drive people and their purchases back to homes or hotels with their purchases as well.

19. VISIT THE ARCADE

Did you know that Providence, Rhode Island is home to the first shopping mall in the United States? Built in 1828, it stretches across one block, with entrances on two parallel streets. Those are a sight to see and one of the best examples of Greek Revival architecture in the entire state.

The Arcade closed down in the late 1990s, abandoned for larger malls out in the suburbs. Its designation as a historic landmark kept it standing, and it finally got a full renovation in the early 21st century. The grand re-opening happened in 2013.

With three floors, you might imagine that this mall has many shops. There are some and the Providence Winter Farmer's Market is held indoors here. However, the top two stories are now small apartments.

The Arcade is home to the Lovecraft Arts and Sciences Council, so it's worth stopping by to see their displays and check out the architecture. There are two restaurants inside as well. The whole mall closes at 6:30 every night except Sunday when it shuts its doors at 3:00.

20. RHODE ISLAND COMICON

If you're in Providence on the first week of November, you will see the city taken over by costumed fans. The Rhode Island Comicon is an enormous event, attracting seventy-thousand attendees each day.

Fans of popular culture book rooms and buy tickets months in advance, some even a year ahead. Be sure to plan your stay accordingly, since hotel spaces are harder to come by at that time.

Even with all the crowding, it's worth visiting Providence and the convention. There's so much to see even if you are not a huge fan of superheroes or comics. There's nothing quite like having a meal or drink beside costumed convention goers or rubbing elbows with the stars of superhero films or action-packed TV shows. If you have children traveling with you, they'll certainly enjoy these extra sights.

21. GET COFFEE MILK

This isn't coffee with milk in it. When you're in Providence, make sure to try this beverage. You can buy it in convenience stores, grocery stores, even many local pharmacies. You can also make it yourself if you are staying some place with a refrigerator.

Coffee milk is what we mean when we say "milkshake" here. It's made just like chocolate or strawberry milk except with coffee flavored syrup added to it before getting shaken or stirred. It's not just for kids, either, though they will enjoy it. Don't worry, the syrup isn't any more caffeinated than the chocolate variety.

If you'd like to make your coffee milk with a kick, try adding vanilla vodka for the best twist on a White Russian ever. I sometimes make mine with a splash of coconut rum, especially over the winter while I dream of summertime.

22. DEL'S FROZEN LEMONADE

Speaking of the summer, another drinkable treat you don't want to miss is Del's. It's something like a slushie but a little more solid and with real fruit in it. It comes in several flavors like watermelon, blueberry, cherry and even grapefruit but lemon is the most popular.

Del's is only available in Rhode Island but not all year. You'll have to enjoy it from May to October if you want to get it from a truck or roadside ice cream stand. Those can be found bear just about any park or outdoor event between May and September. In October, they're a little harder to find unless it's an unseasonably warm day, but they're around.

There's good news for winter travelers staying someplace with a kitchenette, though. You can buy Del's mix at grocery stores in Rhode Island to make with ice in a blender. Like coffee milk, Del's can be enjoyed spiked, if that's your thing. Rum is perfect.

23. CHOW ON CLAM CAKES AND CHOWDER

I bet you're thirsty after reading about those beverages. Here's some food to go with it. Clam cakes are one of the most quintessential New England foods and we've got some of the best here. And where there are cakes, there's chowder.

While it's easier to find them in the summer, the frittered treat is available year-round. Clam cakes are like a savory version of fried dough or Hush Puppies with clams in them. Whether the weather is hot or cold, you'll want a cup of chowder to have on the side.

Rhode Islanders are a bit funny about their chowder. If you order clam chowder, the server will bring a creamy stew with clams, potatoes, and celery, maybe a sprinkle of fresh parsley on top. Some restaurants only have this variety. If you want the tomato-based stuff, be sure to order red or New York chowder. Many restaurants with a selection also have clear chowder where the base is a fish or vegetable broth.

24. TAKE A WALK IN THE PARK

I mentioned the Zoo before, but did you know it's in the middle of a gorgeous park? Roger Williams Park sits on the border of Providence and Cranston, not in walking distance of downtown. Buses run there frequently, however, and it's well worth the trip. You can also hire a car.

You'll find walking trails, monuments like the Temple To Music, themed botanical gardens, boat rides, and a carousel for both kids and adults. There's even a Planetarium. Some areas of the park have seasonal decorations, including spooky Halloween and beautiful Christmas adornments.

The park's website has a listing of events that run year-round. Check to see what coincides with your travel plans but don't worry if nothing in particular is happening that day. It's a gorgeous park with plenty to see on its own at any time of year.

25. GET SPOOKED IN PROVIDENCE

With all the old buildings and antiques around the city, it makes sense to wonder about the paranormal, especially vampires and ghosts. Some locals decided to take that curiosity several steps further.

Rhode Island is home to those guys on the SyFy show, Ghost Hunters. They started investigating reports of paranormal activity in 1990 and kept on going. Because of this, interest in visiting the locations featured on the popular show steadily increased.

If you want to try your hand at investigating ghosts, there are self-directed and guided tours. I prefer the latter because the guides always know new details every time. Some of them even wear costumes and really get into presenting paranormal Providence. Yes, ghost tours are something local Rhode Islanders do, especially in October. We love our local legends, even the scary ones.

26. TRY THE CALAMARI

We like our squid battered and fried here in Providence. Even though it started as an Italian dish, most restaurants have calamari on the menu. Even Japanese places have some version, usually listed as "squid Tempura."

Having calamari is a great way to try eating squid for the first time, especially if you're a bit squeamish. If you stick with the rings instead of the tentacles, you might even forget you are eating squid. Calamari does not taste like onion rings or chicken, instead it's a bit smoky. The texture is slightly chewy.

Calamari can have a variety of flavors and toppings. My favorite is balsamic vinegar and a squeeze of lemon. Others include marinara sauce, spicy mayo, malt vinegar, hot pickled pepper rings, or tartar sauce. I've even seen it with mango chutney. While staying in town, an order of calamari is a must.

27. GET ON THE LOCAL TAP

Most people don't think of beer when they think of Rhode Island but we do have some great local brews. Small microbreweries are nestled in loft spaces at old mills while larger breweries, vineyards, and even a meadery are peppered around the state.

The Trinity Brew House makes all of its beers on the premises in downtown Providence. They serve food to go along with the brews and a handful of soft drinks, too. Even better, you can buy jugs of beer fresh from the tap to take back to your room with you. They stop selling those after nine at night in accordance with liquor store regulations, so be aware that beer take-out isn't on the last call menu.

The Trinity Brew House is located down the street from the Rhode Island Convention Center, the Trinity Reparatory Company, AS220, and Lupo's. It's about two blocks from the Dunkin Donuts Center and the Providence Performing Arts Center. This makes it the perfect meeting spot before or after taking in a show.

28. MAKE A STATE VISIT

If you're even a bit interested in architecture, you must visit the State House. It's located in a vaguely triangular space between Francis Street, Gaspee Street, and Smith Street where the entrance is.

The building itself is a stunning example of neoclassical style, surrounded by a courtyard and a manicured lawn. You can take a look inside when the building is open. On-site parking is for government only but it's an easy walk from the train station, downtown and the Providence Place parking garage.

Both the lawn in back and the courtyard in front have excellent spots to take photos. This government house has free tours every weekday but the hours vary by season. Check the State House website for more details.

29. FASCINATING FALL FOLIAGE

Just about any destination in the northeastern United States offers an opportunity to see beautiful autumn vistas. Providence has several green areas and is no exception. Lots of people come here at this time of year to take a peep at the brightly colored leaves.

If you're visiting in early October, you can expect to see some pretty leaves on the trees but still have some nice weather during the day. The parks are great places to take a stroll but the Hope Village section of Providence is lovely, too, with its tree-lined streets.

The leaf season is over usually by the second week in November. Leaves start changing a little earlier here than in the surrounding states. This gives you time to go north and chase those seasonal changes if you are on a more extended stay in the region.

30. THE PROVIDENCE PERFORMING ARTS CENTER

This is an absolutely gorgeous theatre. It was originally a cinema and opened in 1928. The décor has been kept up since then and it's always a treat just to step inside.

Called the PPAC by locals, this is the venue for touring Broadway shows, comedians, and even concerts. If you have tickets elsewhere or are not looking to sit for a performance, it's still worthwhile to have a look at the place. It's located downtown, not far from many of the other sites mentioned in this book.

If you do want to take in a show at the PPAC, check their website for tickets to events during your stay. Since there are only 3,000 seats, booking early is a good idea. It's easy to reserve tickets online before you even get to the city. You can pick them up at the box office or print them out.

31. DUNKIN DONUTS CENTER

If you thought the PPAC sounded like a big deal, the Dunkin Donuts Center is even bigger. Locals call it "The Dunk" and it's where we have large-scale events like Providence Bruins hockey games, the WWE, Monster Trucks, and figure skating performances like Disney on Ice.

Unlike the PPAC, The Dunk isn't the sort of place to go sightseeing. I recommend it strictly for when you have tickets to a particular event. So many of those booked at the center are worth seeing, though, that there's bound to be something of interest during your stay. The one exception is during Rhode Island ComiCon. That event is so huge, half of it is at The Dunk as well as the Convention Center.

The Dunk is down the street from Providence Place, Trinity Brew House, and across the bridge to Federal Hill. This makes finding dinner to go with your show extremely convenient.

32. TRY TRINITY REPERATORY THEATRE

The Trinity is another gorgeous theater. Built in 1917, it is home to a company which has run professional theater since 1963. All that history adds up to an incredible theatrical presentation from the minute you enter the building.

Students in primary and secondary schools get free passes to this theater, funded by its operation and arts endowments. Supporting Trinity Rep is supporting arts education in the entire state.

Check the Trinity's website for a listing of their seasonal productions. Evening and matinee performances are available but either way, the productions will knock your socks off.

33. FINE ART: THE FESTIVAL BALLET

This ballet troupe has been producing world-class dance art productions for over forty years. Its studio is located in the Hope section of Providence and they do black-box theatre style performance there. However, Festival Ballet also brings such large-scale ensemble shows like The Nutcracker to the Providence Performing Arts Center.

If you're looking for a night of fine performance art with talented dancers, the Festival Ballet has you covered. They run both classic and modern productions so you'll be able to buy tickets to suit your preference.

34. VISIT ART GALLERIES

You can find more than one art gallery in every section of Providence. In fact, there are so many of them that trying to plan a day full of gallery visits can become a challenge in decision-making.

The one can't-miss recommendation I have is the RISD Museum at Chase Center. It's on the border of downtown and College Hill, which makes it centrally located. It's also got seasonal events where alumni sell their work so it's an eclectic mix of styles but never short on quality.

If you don't want to devote a full day to galleries and instead want to see them as you explore other things, apps can come to your rescue. Load up Google Maps or Wayz and take a walk or do lunch. Let the app find the nearest gallery for you. Don't worry if the styles on display aren't your thing. There are plenty more and you get to see the urban-embedded pieces as you go.

35. FUN TIMES AT FOO FEST

The AS220 throws a huge party every year in the middle of August. It's a huge event, like the Godzilla version of a block party. An artist market, live music, food trucks, and more can all be found at Foo Fest.

There are plenty of kid and family-friendly activities as well as stuff to interest single adults. Even sulky teenagers have a good time at Foo Fest. It's got an aura of hipness that only the AS220 can truly convey.

Remember to bring sunscreen, a couple of tote bags, a water bottle, and good walking shoes. With twelve fun-filled hours starting at one in the afternoon, you'll need those for comfort. There's a small admission fee, but it's well worth the cost.

36. ALIGN WITH NECRONOMICON

Every odd year (literally), the weird descends on Providence. I'm not talking about a man with an accordion who parodies popular music (though Weird Al does schedule tour stops here). I mean weird fiction. NecronomiCon.

This is a weekend—long event to celebrate all the literary genres containing strange or horrific elements. Many people consider Edgar Allan Poe as the father of both mystery and horror but H. P. Lovecraft definitely kick-started weird fiction.

If you're looking to be in town during August of an odd-numbered year, consider planning your stay to coincide with the convention. You'll be able to check out not only books, but visual art, music, films, and even attend a costume ball.

37. SEE THE SUMMER CONCERT SERIES

How do we know it's finally summertime in Providence? Del's lemonade is only one piece of the puzzle. We can hear music every other Friday night at Waterplace Park. It's the WBRU Summer Concert Series!

On the first and third Friday during the summer months, two bands play right in the center of downtown Providence. The focus is on local bands, which play all kinds of music, from originals to covers.

Performances are free, start at 7:15, and go until 9. This is perfect timing to have dinner nearby before the show and drinks or dessert somewhere else afterward.

D.R. Perry

38. RIDE A GONDOLA

We're definitely not Venice, but with all the canals that run through Providence, boaters got inspired to provide an alternative method of transportation. You can get a gondola ride through the downtown area.

There are a few companies offering this service and they all have good reviews. My favorite is La Gondola because it has a more Italian flair. Riding in one of the boats is fun for anyone but can be particularly romantic with a special someone.

Be sure to note that gondolas do not run year round. Check to see if they're operating during your stay. They're also not really a good way to get from one section of the city to another, so if you want to get from downtown to Fox Point, you'll want another mode of transportation.

39. PROVIDENCE ARTISANS MARKET

From May to October, there's an open-air market in the Hope section of Providence, right in Lippitt Park. It's got two parts so read straight on through to the next entry if you plan to be in that area on Saturday morning in the sunnier half of the year.

Starting at ten in the morning, artists and crafters from all over the state set up tables and tents with their work. You can find just about anything there, from paintings to pottery. The artists are almost always there with their pieces, so you can ask questions or tell them how much you love what they've made.

They pack up at about the same time as the other half of the market, which is detailed on the next page.

40. HOPE STREET FARMER'S MARKET

Did you choose accommodations with a kitchen? You're in for a treat! Skip the trip to the grocery store and head down to the farmer's market instead. The only thing better than saving money by cooking a meal or two while on vacation is being able to do so with fresh, local ingredients.

Community gardens, Cooperative farms, and orchards or livestock homesteaders with generations of history sit side by side at this market. Fresh produce, dairy and eggs, meat, and spices or preserves are all available.

Even if your crash space doesn't even have a mini-fridge, you can still grab some fresh, seasonal fruit to take with you as you browse the art nearby or enjoy the park. There's always a Del's truck, too, if you need a frosty beverage to wash it down. In winter, you can find the market at The Arcade but without the frozen lemonade.

41. WALKING ON WATERPLACE

You don't actually walk on the water when you go on the RiverWalk, just next to it. I'm talking about a network of cobbled trails which lead up, down, and around the banks of the Providence and Woonasquatucket rivers. The paths are paved with remnants and findings from buildings that are no longer standing in the city.

Along the way, plaques note historic events and buildings that used to sit where you stand. Providence was built literally on the water, a series of platforms hoisted above older structures which got flooded out by a hurricane back in 1938. It's a bit spooky to contemplate but fascinating nonetheless.

When you visit Waterplace Park, remember that it's not just a pretty view with fun events. It's literally immersed in history. If you're especially curious, you can book an informative narrated walking tour.

42. DINING ON THE WATER

All that walking is bound to make a person hungry. Restaurant owners are very smart, so they put plenty of dining options right along the Riverwalk. Some of them even have a direct view of the water, like Jacky's and the Capital Grille.

Steps away, through the Memorial Boulevard underpass, are Luxe Burger and Union Station Brewery for more casual fare. Luxe Burger has vegetarian offerings as well as beef and turkey burgers, with a fun collection of mixed drinks. Union Station often has small acoustic performances and local craft beers from places like The Bucket Brewery.

If you want the best views, however, nothing compares to Skyline at Waterplace. It's posh, so dress accordingly and plan to spend what you'd expect for an upscale dining experience.

43. TAKE A LIGHTHOUSE CRUISE

Did you know that Rhode Island has some of the most interesting historic lighthouses on the East Coast of the United States? You can get a look at them from the deck of a boat on one of Save the Bay's historic lighthouse cruises.

Locals love the shore here and we want it to stay beautiful and fun. That's one huge reason why we love this tour. Proceeds go toward Save The Bay's efforts at keeping Narragansett Bay clean. Full and half day cruises are available, with a 90 minute sunset cruise at the end of the day. Allow at least three hours for the half day tour. I promise you won't get stranded on an island with Gilligan.

The cruise leaves from Fields Point, which is down the street from Johnson & Wales University, not far from Roger Williams Park. This is a year-round activity but outdoor, so dress appropriately for the weather.

44. CHECK OUT HISTORIC CHURCHES

Roger Williams was a rebel for religious freedom. While the rest of New England rocked the Puritanical Protestant vibe, the Rhode Island founder welcomed all sorts. Because of this, Providence is home to the first Baptist Church in America and Newport the first Jewish Synagogue. Since this book focuses on Providence, I'll tell you about what notable houses of worship are here in town.

The First Baptist Church is on the East Side, along with Jewish Synagogue, Temple Beth-El. Downtown, near the border of Federal Hill is the Cathedral of Saints Peter and Paul. Saint Stephen's Episcopal Church is right on the Brown University campus. The First Unitarian Church is on Benefit Street along with some other historic buildings mentioned earlier in this book.

All of these have different hours for services and some are only open to the public by appointment on specific tours. However, you can appreciate the exterior beauty of these beautiful buildings any time.

45. TRAVEL BY THE PROVIDENCE TRAIN STATION

Most people heading in and out of Rhode Island use the airport but the train station has one distinct advantage. It's right in the middle of Providence instead of down in Warwick. Both Amtrak and commuter trains to and from Boston stop there. You can take an Acela from New York City or a regular train from Washington D.C. to get here and then walk to your hotel instead of taking an airport shuttle or hiring a driver.

The station is between Waterplace Park, the State House, and the Providence Place Mall, too, so it's a good way to take a day trip down to the city as part of a longer stay in Boston or up to the nearby city if you want to do something there.

One other reason to visit the station is for breakfast. I'm not kidding. Café La France has great food to start your day, whether you're taking the train or not.

46. GO SKATING

It might seem like there's nothing much to do here in the winter. That's not true at all. We still go out to concerts, galleries, restaurants, and even cruises when it's below freezing. There's one more thing; ice skating.

The name has changed from The Fleet Center to the Alex and Ani Center but it's still the same outdoor urban rink. You can bring your own skates if you want to but they have rentals. It's a fun outdoor activity that you can only do in the wintertime. In summer, Alex and Ani Center is a fountain.

Skating isn't too challenging here, but it's perfect for kids or even adults who are just learning or out of practice like I am. Another great thing to know is that a cup of hot coffee, tea, or hot chocolate is less than a block away in any direction. You'll have your pick of places to get that but North Bakery is right on the rink and you can get a salted caramel cookie, too.

47. ALL THE WAY TO CITY HALL

Providence City Hall is one if the most prominent landmarks you'll find. It dominated Kennedy Plaza with gray granite walls since 1878. At night, the lighting brings out its dramatic lines and rooftop's copper trim.

During the day, you can get inside and have a look at the spacious atrium. Keep your eyes peeled for plaques commemorating famous speeches as well as historical fixtures like the elevator. It's absolutely free to get in, though it's closed on state and national holidays like any other government building.

I mentioned the lighting after dark but there's more than one reason to visit City Hall even when the doors are locked. Haven Brothers, one of the oldest food truck operations, parks outside. You can get mouth-watering sausage, peppers, and onions on a roll. They're open even after last call, and a lifesaver if you are still out and missed dinner.

48. ADORABLE ANIMALS

The Rhode Island Pet Expo happens the first weekend of March. If you're visiting in the spring, it's a great place to see some cute common pets like cats and dogs. Most AKC breeds are represented there.

But like everything else in Providence, this particular pet show has a unique component. There are rare dog breeds as well as other pets, like reptiles and birds, that aren't commonly seen at events like this. The Pet Expo even has pony rides for small children, not something you see every day at an indoor event.

This exposition has an entry fee and is at the Rhode Island Convention Center. It's been running since 1994 with no sign of shutting down. If you're coming in the fall instead, the Rhode Island Pet Show runs during the second weekend of November, right after Rhode Island Comicon. You could see both events if you plan accordingly.

49. GET OUT OF TOWN

Why would you want to leave Providence when the whole point is to visit? Well, we've got a second city to explore in this state. And people think we're tiny. Newport is home to just as many amazing sights, sounds, and suppers as you can find in Providence. But that story could take up a second volume.

If you're interested in visiting Newport, it's much easier to get there from Providence than it used to be. We've got the Seastreak Ferry that leaves from Fox Point. It's a short jaunt, inexpensive, and comfortable. The best part is, you don't need a car in either downtown area, so this ferry saves you the hassle of an auto rental and an hour driving across toll bridges.

Even if you don't want to spend the day in Newport, a ride on the ferry is a good way to get out on the water and see the bay without a narrated tour. If lighthouse facts are not your thing this is a decent and shorter alternative to Save The Bay's Lighthouse Tour.

50. HIT THE BOOKS

The Providence Public Library has served the city for almost one hundred and forty years. It's also been the venue of choice for several weddings because of its elegant design. I'm there frequently, getting out of the house for some time writing around books and convenient research resources.

Like many other buildings in Providence, the library has its own unique style. You've likely noticed a trend by now, that anything enduring in this city stands apart in some way.

The library, like the citizens it serves, is eclectic in and of itself but also in relation to the rest of the surrounding structures. At first glance, some might think that Providence is a mish-mosh of skyline shapes and styles, a mixed bag like a Halloween candy haul or Forrest Gump's box of chocolates.

You never know what you'll get when you turn a corner, enter a building, or turn over an antique in this town. But that only means there's something for everyone.

Providence is a glory of individualism, a whole greater than the expected sum of its parts. And that's exactly why I love it here.

>TOURIST

D.R. Perry

TOP REASONS TO BOOK THIS TRIP

Cuisine: We've got some of the best and most diverse collection of restaurants here in Providence. You can have a different style of food every night for a month at least.

History: Everything's historical. As one of the thirteen original Colonies in the United States, there's a lot to learn as well as see. You can also take some of that history home with you in the form of antiques or local art honoring the past.

Quirky Culture: Rhode Island is unique, with so many little details that make it a truly special place.

D.R. Perry

> TOURIST
GREATER THAN A TOURIST

Visit GreaterThanATourist.com:

http://GreaterThanATourist.com

Sign up for the Greater Than a Tourist Newsletter:

http://eepurl.com/cxspyf

Follow us on Facebook:

https://www.facebook.com/GreaterThanATourist

Follow us on Pinterest:

http://pinterest.com/GreaterThanATourist

Follow us on Instagram:

http://Instagram.com/GreaterThanATourist

D.R. Perry

> TOURIST
GREATER THAN A TOURIST

Please leave your honest review of this book on Amazon and Goodreads. Thank you. We appreciate your positive and constructive feedback. Thank you.

Author Name Here

NOTES

Made in the USA
Middletown, DE
09 October 2018